W9-BNI-771

Dear Parents and Educators,

Welcome to Penguin Young Readers! As parents and educators, you know that each child develops at his or her own pace—in terms of speech, critical thinking, and, of course, reading. Penguin Young Readers recognizes this fact. As a result, each Penguin Young Readers book is assigned a traditional easy-to-read level (1–4) as well as a Guided Reading Level (A–P). Both of these systems will help you choose the right book for your child. Please refer to the back of each book for specific leveling information. Penguin Young Readers features esteemed authors and illustrators, stories about favorite characters, fascinating nonfiction, and more!

Baby Meerkats

LEVEL 3

GUIDED READING LEVEL M

This book is perfect for a **Transitional Reader** who:

- can read multisyllable and compound words;
- can read words with prefixes and suffixes;
- is able to identify story elements (beginning, middle, end, plot, setting, characters, problem, solution); and
- can understand different points of view.

Here are some **activities** you can do during and after reading this book:

- Comprehension: After reading the book, answer the following questions.
  - What are baby meerkats called?
  - What do baby meerkats do when they first leave their burrows?
  - What kinds of jobs can members of a meerkat family have?
  - What is mobbing?
  - What do meerkats eat?
- Research: Meerkats live in the Kalahari Desert in southern Africa. Find the Kalahari Desert on a map. Go to the library or use the Internet to learn about other animals that live there.

Remember, sharing the love of reading with a child is the best gift you can give!

—Bonnie Bader, EdM
Penguin Young Readers program

*Penguin Young Readers are leveled by independent reviewers applying the standards developed by Irene Fountas and Gay Su Pinnell in *Matching Books to Readers: Using Leveled Books in Guided Reading*, Heinemann, 1999.

To Kim Whaley and Nancy Essid, both librarians and friends, and to the First UU women's circle, for providing me with a safe community—GLC

For Eamon, Miles, Reece, Neve, Kieran, and Meghan, with love—RC

Penguin Young Readers
Published by the Penguin Group
Penguin Group (USA) Inc., 375 Hudson Street, New York, New York 10014, USA
Penguin Group (Canada), 90 Eglinton Avenue East, Suite 700, Toronto, Ontario M4P 2Y3, Canada
(a division of Pearson Penguin Canada Inc.)
Penguin Books Ltd, 80 Strand, London WC2R 0RL, England
Penguin Ireland, 25 St Stephen's Green, Dublin 2, Ireland (a division of Penguin Books Ltd)
Penguin Group (Australia), 707 Collins Street, Melbourne, Victoria 3008, Australia
(a division of Pearson Australia Group Pty Ltd)
Penguin Books India Pvt Ltd, 11 Community Centre, Panchsheel Park, New Delhi—110 017, India
Penguin Group (NZ), 67 Apollo Drive, Rosedale, Auckland 0632, New Zealand
(a division of Pearson New Zealand Ltd)
Penguin Books, Rosebank Office Park, 181 Jan Smuts Avenue, Parktown North 2193, South Africa
Penguin China, B7 Jaiming Center, 27 East Third Ring Road North,
Chaoyang District, Beijing 100020, China

Penguin Books Ltd, Registered Offices: 80 Strand, London WC2R 0RL, England

All rights reserved. No part of this book may be reproduced, scanned, or distributed in any printed or electronic form without permission. Please do not participate in or encourage piracy of copyrighted materials in violation of the author's rights. Purchase only authorized editions.

Text copyright © 2010 by Ginjer L. Clarke. Illustrations copyright © 2010 by Robbin Cuddy.
All rights reserved. First published in 2010 by Grosset & Dunlap, an imprint of Penguin Group (USA) Inc.
Published in 2013 by Penguin Young Readers, an imprint of Penguin Group (USA) Inc.,
345 Hudson Street, New York, New York 10014. Manufactured in China.

Library of Congress Control Number: 2009036050

ISBN 978-0-448-45106-0 10 9 8 7 6 5 4 3 2 1

ALWAYS LEARNING PEARSON

PENGUIN YOUNG READERS
LEVEL 3
TRANSITIONAL READER

Baby MeerKats

by Ginjer L. Clarke
illustrated by Robbin Cuddy

Penguin Young Readers
An Imprint of Penguin Group (USA) Inc.

A family of little animals sits together quietly to watch the sunset. They are meerkats. They live in the Kalahari Desert in southern Africa. Each family of meerkats has an

older female who is in charge. She is their leader.

Tonight, she is having babies. The whole meerkat family will help her take care of the babies.

The meerkats go into their burrow. A *burrow* is a hole underground with many tunnels and rooms. The rooms are cool in the day when the desert is hot and warm at night when it gets cold.

The whole meerkat family sleeps in a cozy pile in a big room. But the meerkat mother rests in a room by herself tonight on a nest made of grass. She needs a quiet place to have her babies.

The meerkats wake up when they hear soft crying noises.

Mew! Mew! Three new meerkat babies have been born into the family. They are called *pups* or *kits*.

Meerkat pups are so small that you could fit one in your hands.

They cannot see and have no fur. The meerkat mother cuddles her pups to keep them warm. They drink their mother's milk. This helps them to grow bigger.

In the morning, the mother needs to find food right away. It takes a lot of work to feed and care for the pups, so the whole family has to help.

The other female meerkats and some male meerkats take turns watching the pups.

They are called *babysitters*. There is a babysitter with the baby meerkats at all times. The mother cannot leave to find food until a babysitter comes. Sometimes a babysitter does not eat anything for a whole day!

The pups stay in the burrow until they are two weeks old. Now they are bigger, and their eyes are open.

They explore the tunnels until they find a way out. They poke their heads up and see the sky for the first time.

The baby meerkats can go outside during the day. But they do not go far. A babysitter is always nearby to watch over them.

The baby meerkats live in the burrow where they were born until they are about four weeks old.

Now they are ready to eat real food. Their babysitter digs in the ground with her long claws. She finds a wiggly grub worm.

One of the pups smells the grub. *Squish!* She bites into it and gulps it down. The other two pups are also given grubs for their first meal. They like this tasty treat.

The rest of the meerkat family hunts for prey in the desert. The mother meerkat leads them to good digging spots.

Sniff! Their noses are small, but they still have a super sense of smell. They dig holes quickly to find food that moves fast underground.

Meerkats have pointed snouts with lots of small, sharp teeth to help them chew quickly. Meerkats eat insects, lizards, spiders, mice, small snakes—and even scorpions!

Crunch! A meerkat bites off a scorpion's stinger. Then he munches on the rest of its body.

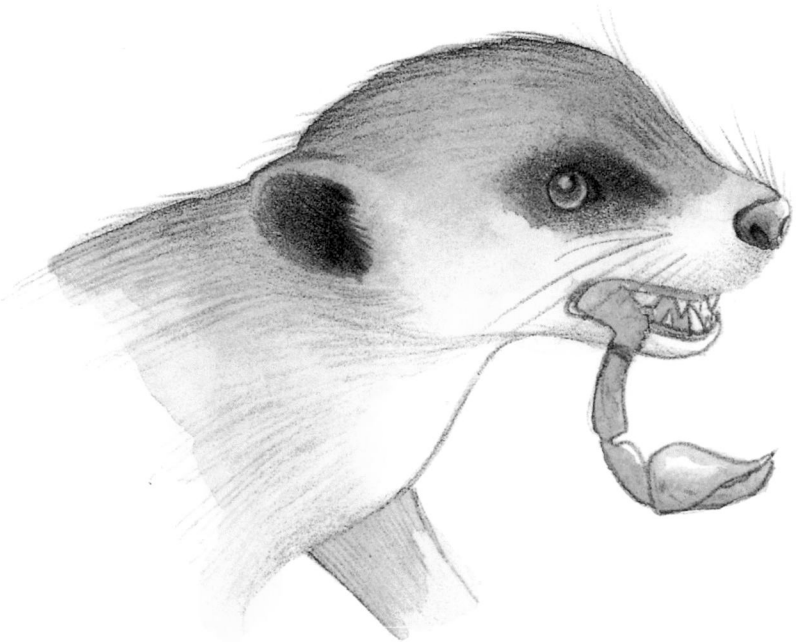

Meerkats eat many times a day, but they do not get very big. They weigh about two pounds. They grow up to be about 12 inches tall when standing. That is only as long as a ruler!

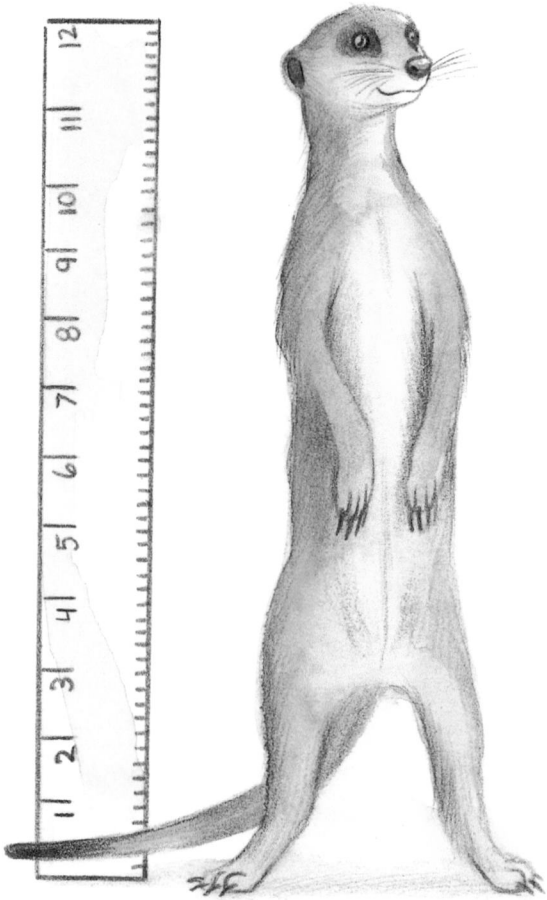

Meerkats have circles of dark hair around their big, black eyes. It looks like they are wearing sunglasses! The dark circles bounce light away from the meerkats' eyes. This helps them see in the sun, just like sunglasses help you.

In the early morning, meerkats watch the sunrise together. They sit up on their back legs and face the sun in a line. They use their long tails to help them balance.

The desert is cold in the morning and at night but hot during the day. Meerkats have fur on their backs but dark skin on their bellies. The skin soaks up the sun's heat and helps them get warm fast.

Now that they are warm, the meerkats get to work. There can be up to 30 meerkats in a family. Each meerkat has a job. Some dig out the burrow. Others hunt for prey.

Just like some meerkats are babysitters, others are teachers who

teach the pups how and where to find food.

A few meerkats are sentries (say: SEHN-treez), or guards. They look for danger all around. Meerkats are true team players!

These meerkat sentries are standing watch on a big rock. They look on the ground for jackals, foxes, or wildcats. They stare at the sky for eagles, hawks, or vultures. These animals eat meerkats.

Bark! Bark! The sentries spot a Martial eagle flying overhead. Sentries have different calls for predators in the sky or on the ground. *BARK! BARK!* They bark louder as the predator gets closer.

The meerkats hear the warning. They run quickly into a bolt-hole to hide from the eagle. *Bolt-holes* are like burrows, but they are much smaller. There are lots of bolt-holes wherever meerkats hunt.

Scritch! Scratch! The sentries scratch in the dirt to make big clouds of dust. The dust confuses the eagle, so it cannot find the meerkats. They all get away safely. The sentries save the day!

The meerkats work all morning until the sun gets too hot. Then the meerkat mother tells the other meerkats to stop digging.

It is time to head home to check on the baby meerkats and bring them some food. The whole meerkat family rests in the cool burrow to get out of the heat. A sentry watches over them as they sleep soundly.

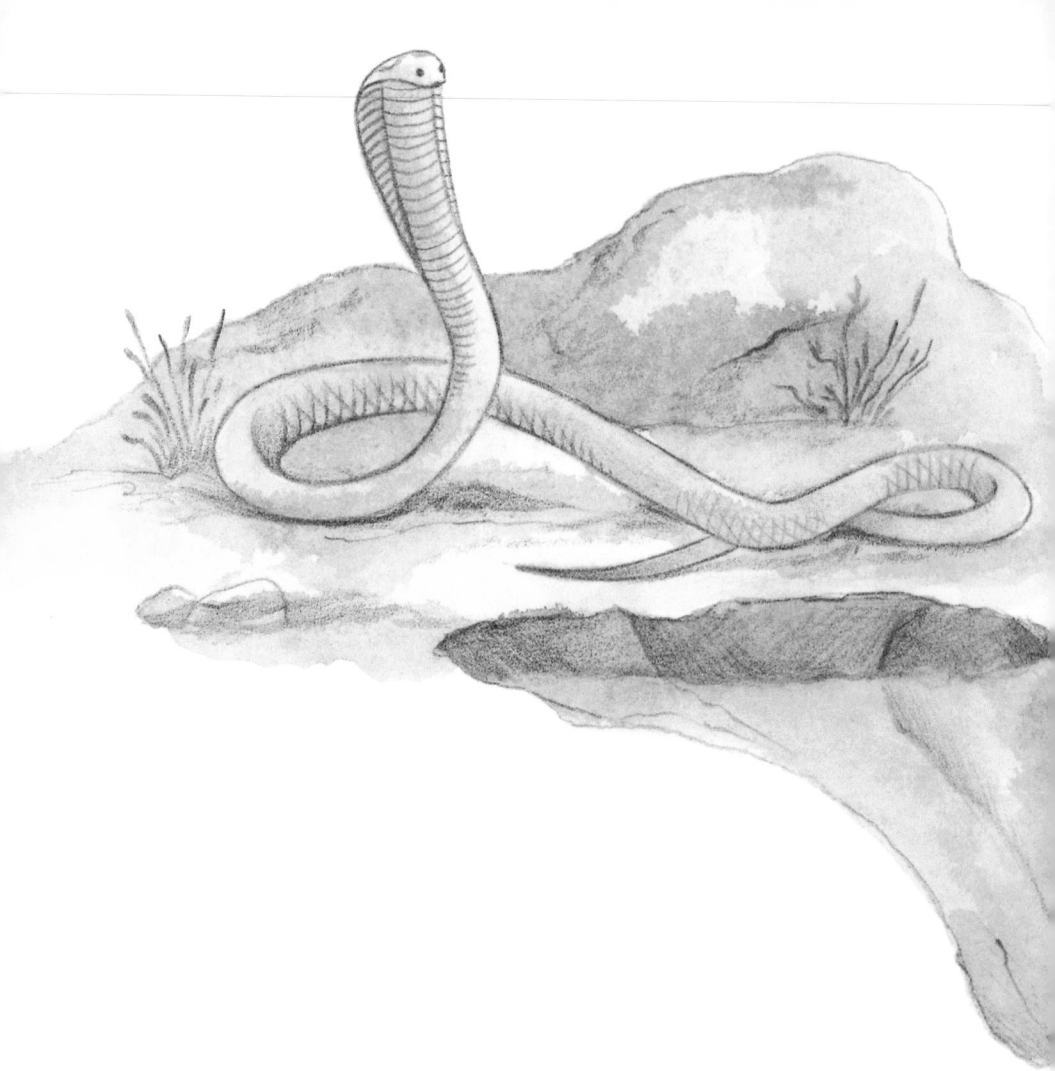

In the late afternoon, the desert cools down. The meerkats wake up.

Uh-oh! The meerkats smell a snake outside the burrow. It is a Cape cobra—one of their worst enemies.

Meerkats sometimes share their burrows with rodents, squirrels, and yellow mongooses. But they do not like snakes. Some snakes hurt or kill meerkats when they bite.

The meerkats all run outside. *Hiss-s-s-s!* The cobra moves toward the meerkats. The meerkat family forms a circle around the cobra. They try to scare the cobra so it will go away. This is called *mobbing*.

The meerkats puff up their fur and raise their tails. This makes them look bigger. They bob their heads as if they are going to bite. They jump, growl, and spit. Finally, the cobra slithers off. Hooray for the meerkats!

Enemies often come back once they find a meerkat burrow. So the mother meerkat moves her family to another burrow nearby.

Yip! Yip! She calls to the meerkats, and everyone follows her.

The pups are growing, but they cannot run fast yet. The babysitters hold the pups gently in their mouths to carry them to the new burrow.

Outside their new home, the pups play with their older siblings and cousins. They chase, climb, and pretend to fight one another. Playing helps them learn skills they will use as they grow.

The pups also learn how to keep one another clean. Meerkats have a lot of bugs, like fleas, in their fur. They use their claws and teeth to pick and bite the bugs off of their fur. Then they eat the bugs!

While the young meerkats play, the older meerkats dig. Desert sand and dirt move a lot, so the holes and tunnels in the new burrow have to be dug out.

Whoosh! The meerkats send sand and dirt flying everywhere.

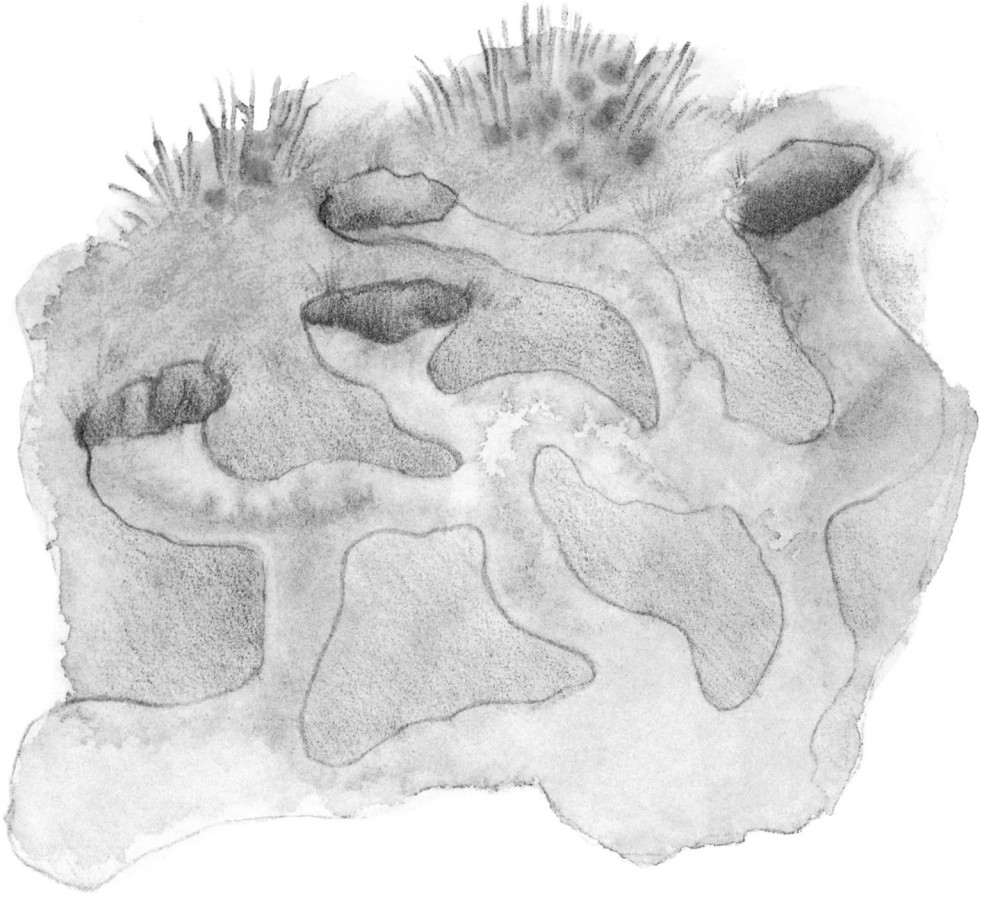

A meerkat family has a few different burrows to live in. Meerkats move around in their territory (say: TAYR-uh-tor-ee) that is several miles long. Sometimes, different families fight over their territories.

Squeak! A sentry sends a warning. A family of meerkats is coming, and they are ready to fight. They think this is their territory. Both meerkat families face off with their tails held high.

The meerkats rock back and forth. This is called a war dance.

Charge! The meerkats bounce toward one another and fight. They hiss, bite, and scratch. The other meerkats get hurt. They give up and run away.

A few more months go by. The pups are four months old. Each pup gets a teacher. The teacher shows the pup how and where to find food and how to watch for danger.

One teacher catches a big lizard. The lizard is hurt but not dead. The teacher drops the lizard, so the pup can practice hunting. The pup plays with the lizard.

Whoops! The lizard got away. The pup will try harder next time.

After more practice, the pups start hunting on their own. One pup finds a millipede. He bites it in half and eats its juicy guts. *Slurp!*

Another pup digs a deep hole. She sticks her head and body all the way into the hole. Suddenly, she pops up. She found a big beetle, but it snapped her on the nose! *Ouch!*

Meerkats have to work hard to find food in the dry desert. But when the rain comes, the grasses grow tall. There is food and water for everyone.

At six months old, the pups are almost fully grown. They can hunt with the adults.

Sometimes the baby meerkats get lost in the tall grasses. The meerkat mother climbs up into a tree to look for them. She spots them and chirps to tell them to go home. Another busy day is over.

The desert is a difficult place for meerkats to live. But by working together, the family keeps growing and stays out of danger. Meerkats may be small, but they stand up tall.